How t Codependency And Set Boundaries

A Quick Guide to Break Free from The Codependent Cycle

BY

Bob Scott

Copyright

All rights reserved. No part of this publication **HOW TO STOP CODEPENDENCY AND SET BOUNDARIES** may be reproduced, stored in a retrieval system or transmitted in any form or by any means, electronic, mechanical, photocopying, recording, and scanning without permission in writing by the author.

Printed in the United States of America
© 2019 by Bob Scott

Double Portion Publishers

USA | CANADA

Table of Contents

Introduction 5

CHAPTER ONE: Causes of Co-dependency 9

CHAPTER TWO: Negative Effects of Co-dependency 13

CHAPTER THREE: The Importance of Setting Boundaries 19

CHAPTER FOUR: Breaking Co-dependency in a Relationship 23

CHAPTER FIVE: How to Set Healthy Boundaries 30

CHAPTER SIX: How to Not Be Co-dependent .. 37

CHAPTER SEVEN: 7 Steps for Breaking the Co-dependency Cycle 41

Other Books by The Same Author 72

Introduction

Co-dependency is one of those words that get thrown around so often you assume you know the meaning but whose interpretation may be different from what you thought. Let's start from the basics.

Co-dependency is a relationship between two people in which one individual (the co-dependent) desires to and thrive on being needed and the other person (the enabler) relies on the co-dependent. Co-dependency can exist between family members, friends, or love partners but is usually denoted by a form of abuse (physical, psychological, or emotional) or another.

In a normal, healthy relationship, the two individuals rely on each other for care, love, and support as they both contribute to the relationship. But in a co-dependent relationship, the co-dependent *has* to be needed. If they are not, co-dependents feel worthless and despair creeps in. Without being needed, this person believes their very life has no purpose.

And while people in normal relationships value each other, they still have other interests such as their career, recreational activities, hobbies, and other friendships. This is not the same in co-dependency as a co-dependent is jealous about their relationship with the enabler. They have no interest or outside activities as they dedicate their lives into pleasing the enabler. This means a co-dependent does not live a full life. Things such as career, friendships, hobbies, and every other thing that makes a perfectly rounded individual is abandoned or unprioritized.

It may not be easy to recognize co-dependency in a relationship. After all, we all want to be loved and cared for and seeing someone dedicated to their partners might make you think the relationship a perfect one. Here are typical symptoms of co-dependency:

1) A co-dependent get joy and satisfaction only from serving the enabler. Nothing outside of this gives them happiness.
2) A co-dependent may be aware that their partner continually hurt them,

yet they will remain in the relationship.
3) A co-dependent will go to any length to satisfy the enabler.
4) A co-dependent lives in a state of anxiety, always anxious to please and stay in the good books of the enabler.
5) A co-dependent dedicate their life and energy to giving their partner whatever they desire.
6) They ignore their own needs and have feelings of guilt whenever they do not.

When you observe these signs, recognize that such a relationship is co-dependent. Now as an observer looking in, you may try to advise the co-dependent to leave and take charge of their own life. Do not be surprised if they do not, most co-dependents will never leave as their feeling of self-worth as a human is tied to the sacrifices they make in the relationship.

CHAPTER ONE: Causes of Co-dependency

No one was born as a co-dependent. It is a learned behavior, an adaptation for survival by victims of abuse or people that have undergone emotional difficulties. Any of these can lead to a co-dependency.

> a) Dysfunctional parental relationships: When a child grows up in a family where their own needs are seen as less important than that of the parent(s) and the child ended up focusing on the wants and needs of the parent(s), a co-dependency results.
> A parent with an addiction (drugs or alcohol) or emotional immaturity may blame their child for their problems or label the child selfish if they ever want anything for themselves. Such children grow up ignoring their own needs and always seeking out co-dependent relationships.
> b) Living with an ill family member: Illnesses take tolls on people and it is especially draining on caregivers and children. In some cases, a child may

be forced into the role of a caregiver especially if a parent is mentally or physically ill. This almost always results in the child becoming co-dependent.

Living with an ill family member does not often result in co-dependency but if the sick person begrudges the child or caretaker opportunities to do other things outside of taking care of them, guilt them into giving up friends or extra-curricular activities, it is quite likely that a co-dependency will develop.

c) Living in an abusive household: Abuse of various kinds may result in psychological problems one of which is co-dependency. An abused child may learn to repress their feelings as a sort of coping mechanism against the abuse. The child may grow up to believe that they do not matter, their feelings don't count and that their true purpose is to please others no matter how draining or debasing that may be. It is also possible for an abused child or teenager to take it as normal. Such people will seek out only this type of relationships when they grow up.

CHAPTER TWO: Negative Effects of Co-dependency

There is no advantage to co-dependency. It should never exist in a normal, healthy relationship. Its negative effect is more often felt by the co-dependent, who gives up any semblance of normal life in order to serve the enabler. It can affect both the enabler and co-dependent in different ways.

Health problems.

A co-dependent never express their feelings in a relationship. Since they need other people to need them, co-dependent are afraid of scaring away the enabler and would rather maintain the status quo than say how they feel. The result is that they bottle up their feelings without any form of expression. This makes them susceptible to different health problems including anxiety, depression, panic attacks, etc.

Self-abandonment.

The healthy way of dealing with painful events is to allow yourself to feel them. But a co-dependent not only refuses to feel but may also refuse assistance from others. They do not want to be taken care of which lead to greater physical and mental exhaustion.

Self-neglect.

The Good Book says love your neighbor as yourself. This does not hold for co-dependent relationships. While a co-dependent will go to great lengths to take care of the other person, their own get neglected,

Inability to stay alone.

A co-dependent needs to take care of others. This makes them unable to stay alone as they never know what to do with themselves if there is no one to fuss over. The result is developing damaging relationships with unsuitable people all in an attempt to have someone to care for. Most will enter abusive relationships and suffer all kinds of degradation.

Inability to accept help.

Co-dependents will give and give, often at great costs to their physical, mental, and emotional health but find it difficult to accept help from other people. They find it difficult to leave the caregiver role and fear that others may become resentful if they accept the help being offered.

Inability to set boundaries.

Setting and maintaining healthy boundaries is crucial to self-respect and giving others respect. Boundaries are invisible lines that determine what you accept and how others get to treat your space, body, money, needs, feelings, etc. and how you, in turn, treat theirs. But co-dependents find it difficult to set boundaries so they get cheated, inconvenienced, and used which leads them into depression and other psychological problems.

Controlling behavior.

It may seem counterintuitive when co-dependents are described as controlling. After all, they give so much to their partner and others. But therein lies the crux of this behavior; they can get so obsessed with helping others that they would want others to do exactly as they recommended. Any deviation from their plan makes them unhappy. To get away from the rigid way of living their lives, co-dependents may turn to alcohol or other substances and abuse them.

Poor communication.

Because co-dependents never express their feelings, they don't tell others the truth for fear of getting people upset. So even when they aren't okay with a situation, they may believe they have no choice than to accept it. This may lead to a build-up of resentment that their thoughts are not valued, even though they never expressed the thoughts in the first place.

Depending on the validation of others. One characteristic of all co-dependents is the need to be accepted by others. They suffer from the fear of getting rejected and will, therefore, do anything to retain the affection and acceptance of an enabler. As they have no identity of their own but rather attach it to their relationship with others (for example Zack's wife, Kavaa's mum, Daddy's little girl, etc.), they only enjoy a sense of fulfillment when in a relationship. It becomes very easy for them to get stuck in abusive relationships.

Living a life of denial.

Co-dependency remains a problem because sufferers never accept that they have a problem. Denial forms a huge part of their lives; they deny accepting that the relationship is unhealthy, deny their own needs, deny that they get exhausted, etc. Even when they get to their breaking point, they still do not accept help from others and sooner or later, burn out.

CHAPTER THREE: The Importance of Setting Boundaries

Human beings are social animals and need relationships and a sense of community in order to function fully. As wonderful as relationships and interconnectedness are, it is still important that you protect your own individualism while others do the same. Without this, a relationship cannot be truly deemed healthy.

Loving someone involves giving your time, resources, money, efforts, and many more things needed to make their lives easier but care should be taken so that you do not get lost in meeting someone else's desire and neglecting your own needs. Here are valid reasons why you should stop co-dependency and allow for healthy boundaries in relationships.

1. **Boundaries allow for individuality:** Every single human on earth is unique, even identical twins are not completely the same in behavior, thoughts, and inclinations. Co-dependency strips the co-dependent of his/her individuality as they spend their lives taking care of others, listening for cues of

dissatisfaction. It leads to loss of self, feelings of guilt, stress, and feelings of not being enough.

Having boundaries allows no room for co-dependency. It will make every individual take responsibility for the way they live.

2. **Boundaries prevent you from being taken advantage of:** In relationships where there are no boundaries, there is room for one party to take advantage of the other party's love and affection. But with boundaries, you realize that every act of kindness and sacrifice your partner, father, sister, or friend did is out of love and not because it is your right. A mother will be able to live her life without giving up the things that matter to her just to satisfy her family.

3. **Boundaries give you the opportunity to enjoy talents or interests outside of a relationship:** In co-dependency, the co-dependent does not have the time or opportunity to explore talents or

interests that the enabler is not interested in. this is because every free time is spent tending to the enabler and ensuring their comfort. With boundaries in place, you can take up hobbies that your partner is not interested in without feelings of guilt.

4. **Boundaries prevent you from wallowing in resentment:** Relationships where there are no established boundaries cannot be happy or healthy. At least one partner will be miserable or resentful. One partner may likely go further and further down the path of addiction and destruction as they are enabled and have every whim taken care of.

   With boundaries, there is an opportunity for both parties to grow and improve, take responsibility, listen to corrections, and generally become better humans.

CHAPTER FOUR: Breaking Co-dependency in a Relationship

The moment you realize that you are in a co-dependent relationship, you are on your way to healing. To break this cycle of co-dependency, you need to learn to value yourself and treat yourself with respect. You realize that you can walk away from a relationship because you are enough, because your needs are valid because you do not have to sacrifice your own happiness in order to make someone else happy.

Here are ways in which you can put a stop to co-dependency and live the full life you truly deserve:

i. **Realize that a relationship is not what guarantees happiness:** In a co-dependent relationship, you may be used to sacrificing yourself for your partner's dreams and goals. You may give up on a lot of things that give you fulfillment just to be able to hold on to a partner and the relationship. Because you have bought into the lie that your life is incomplete without the other person, that your happiness is tied to that person being in your life, you may put all your resources into a relationship that gives you nothing in return.

You need to get to the realization that a relationship is just a part of your life but not the main thing, definitely not the glue that holds your person together. Look at your other relationships with new eyes, start seeing your friends as an important part of your life. Value your ambitions and devote time to working on them too. Take time out for hobbies and recreation. If your partner begrudges you doing other things that bring you happiness, then you need to get out of the relationship totally. When you meet someone new, evaluate them and your reasons for being with them first. Be sure you want them as a part of a healthy relationship and not just to meet an emotional need.

ii. **Realize that you can derive emotional intimacy from non-romantic relationships:** It is very easy for lonely people to get caught in the trap of co-dependency. When you have solid friendships outside of a romantic relationship, you will hardly fall into co-dependency, find friends that you can open up to, people you can show your vulnerability to and who will support you. You will find that friendships can be emotionally fulfilling and that when you have people that have your back, you will have healthy self-esteem that prevents you from allowing yourself to be treated like a second class citizen in a relationship. You will find the love of a partner as an extra and not the sustenance you need for life.

iii. **Realize that it is okay to be alone:** If you ended a co-dependent relationship, you should take as much time as you need to get to know yourself. Realize that there is nothing wrong with being alone and take time to enjoy yourself, do the things that make you happy and make time for self-care. You need to know yourself before you can set healthy boundaries and completely let go of co-dependency.

You may even find out that you actually love being by yourself and can use that time for self-development, learning a craft, or pursuing a hobby. Once you are at this stage, you will not go into a relationship just to stop being by yourself but actually choose a relationship where you will both give and take care of each other.

iv. **Never ignore other relationships when you fall in love:** If you are one of those people who forget other friendships the moment a new love interest appears on the horizon, you may find yourself moving into a co-dependency quite easily. When you cancel plans made with friends just to spend a few more hours with a partner, when you opt out of that long-planned trip with the girls because you don't want to leave your partner alone for a few days, you are creating a distance and telling them that they are not important to you.

The moment you begin to give up on those other important parts of your life, you have begun a gradual slide to giving up on yourself in other ways. You will start going out of your way to please a partner, back down from talking about issues that you are uncomfortable with, get used to having your opinions ignored by your partner, etc.

At every stage in life, you need non-romantic support to keep you grounded and to enable you to enjoy life in full.

v. **Love yourself first:** Co-dependents go to great lengths to please their partners because they crave love so much and want their partner to love them. They believe that by sacrificing themselves and the things that matter to them, they will get loved in return.

This is the wrong way to go about looking for love as you will never be truly loved by someone else unless you love yourself first. Make yourself a priority, recognize that you are worthy of love, attention, and affection. If you see yourself this way, it will be difficult for you to stay in a co-dependent relationship because of the wrong notion that no one else will love you.

So love yourself enough to know that you are worth so much, that you bring great value to any relationship and deserve respect from your partner. It will become easy for you to recognize narcissists in your life and cut them off without apology. You will also know that you do not need a relationship to validate your worth, you can then get out of a relationship that is not giving you joy.

CHAPTER FIVE: How to Set Healthy Boundaries

There are no healthy relationships without boundaries. It helps us know what our limits are towards protecting our space and peace of mind and prevent us from infringing on other people's space as well.

You may think that having boundaries is not necessary in relationships with family and friends but this is not true. Since it is possible for co-dependency to develop among family members or friends, setting boundaries is essential. Interested in knowing how to set boundaries? Read on.

1. **Identify your limits.** An axiom says, "there is no crime where there is no law." You cannot have boundaries if you do not identify a particular limit beyond which you will not go or allow other people to pass. Identify your limits in all regards—emotionally, mentally, physically, and in any other way that matter to you. Know the things you can tolerate without having to suppress your feelings or emotions. Identify the things that you are uncomfortable

doing (even if the people around you are quite comfortable with it) and accept your own limits.
2. **Get in touch with your feelings.** Get to know yourself so that you do not suppress how you feel just to make other people comfortable. The moment you start feeling discomfited about a situation or issue, you are already allowing your boundaries to be run over. Resentment is a cue to let you know that you have ignored your boundaries. You get resentful probably as a result of being taken advantage of (you may want to be a good wife and compromise on things that matter a great deal to you) or someone else forcing their views, opinions, or desires on you.
3. **Be straightforward.** You may need to cut through the fluff and just spell out your boundaries to people. This is especially important when dealing with people of a different personality than yours. They may not understand the subtle communication of your boundaries and may keep breaching

it out of ignorance. Do not feel weird if you have to have a clear-cut conversation with people about what your limits are.

4. **Boundaries are your right.** You may feel odd about setting boundaries in relationships where you've not had any before. If you do, understand that having and maintaining healthy boundaries is your right. It is essential to your physical, mental, and emotional health and almost as important as oxygen. You may be afraid of other people's reactions when you choose to enforce your boundaries or feel guilty because you have to say no to family. Recognize that guilt, doubt, and trepidation all lie on the other side of self-respect. As long as you allow them to determine your actions, you will always give room for others to treat you without regard. Stop getting roped into the cliché "If you are a good son/daughter, you would...". Maintain boundaries, they are your right.

5. **Be self-aware.** It is easy to keep letting go of your boundaries if you have allowed yourself to be treated as less than an equal in relationships. Self-awareness quickly lets you know when you start sliding and stop sustaining set boundaries. Self-awareness will quickly let you know when something is 'off'. Ask yourself questions about why you are feeling stressed, or unhappy or resentful. Then decide on what to do about it. Pro tip: Never allow people to run over your boundaries once you've made them aware of them. If you allow them once, they will probably expect you to do so again.
6. **Look back, then around you.** If you were the caretaker or the 'mother' of the house while growing up, you might have gotten used to taking care of others and forgetting about your own needs. You might even believe that being emotionally or physically exhausted is normal. You need to realize that no relationship should get you drained. Also that any

relationship you are in should restore and take care of you even as you do for them.

Consider your primary environment. If the people around you allow certain liberty that breaches your own boundaries, it may be difficult being the odd one out when you want to maintain boundaries. If you cannot change your environment, remember that your boundaries are important and continue enforcing them.

7. **Prioritize self-care.** Remember this always: you come first. When you put yourself first, you will find it easier to set and maintain boundaries that guarantee your peace of mind. This means you will recognize that your feelings are valid, you will not force yourself to put up with an invasion of your personal space that feels uncomfortable to you, you will not ignore calling out someone that is abusive towards you.

8. **Be assertive:** Setting boundaries is quite useless if you are not going to

enforce it. This means that you let people know when they have crossed a boundary. You can only do this by being assertive and ready to have uncomfortable conversations with people.

CHAPTER SIX: How to Not Be Co-dependent

While the disadvantages to co-dependency are numerous, it is quite easy to fall into co-dependency with some family relationships. Here are ways to make sure you do not slide into co-dependency:

A. Give because you want to: To love unconditionally is to do things to make other people's lives better because you truly want to. You will give freely without sacrifice and make sure you take care of yourself while doing the same. You will not give up hobbies or stop pursuing a talent, neither will you neglect your job or friends because you want to make your partner happy.

B. Address hurtful behavior: When you get hurt by the actions of the other person, you should be ready to talk about it. Take time to calm down first and then determine the cause of that hurtful behavior. When you know the cause, it becomes easy to let them know how it hurts you and how they can stop doing that.

C. Be certain of what your personal boundaries: Let your boundaries be very clear to both family and friends. Also, be sure that you respect other people's boundaries too. If any action hurts you, you can then determine if you are the one trying to cross the other person's boundaries or whether they are invading yours. Then if they are running over yours, you can put your foot down and refuse to cave in and if you are the culprit, you get to back off.

D. Stop any controlling behavior: If you are the type that always wants to have the last word, you may be closer to co-dependency than you thought. If you want everything to be the way you want it, without taking into consideration the other person, realize that it is a co-dependent trait and stop it.

E. Do not insult your partner or family in an argument: When you are unhappy with a situation, do not name call. Rather, explain how you feel without using any foul language.

The key to stopping co-dependency is to value yourself. When you know you are worth much, you will not accept it when someone treats you with disrespect or ignores your feelings. It will make it easy to cut off people that repeatedly treat you without regard before they start damaging your self-esteem. Know that you do not need to be in a romantic relationship to enjoy emotional intimacy, that there is nothing wrong with being alone, and that a healthy relationship will not want you to give up the things that make you happy.

CHAPTER SEVEN: 7 Steps for Breaking the Co-dependency Cycle

Breaking the cycle of co-dependency is never easy. Whether as a co-dependent or the enabler, getting healing and forming healthy relationships will take work and a lot of effort. It starts with the determination to place value on yourself and regain your sense of self.

Here are seven steps that will help you leave a life of co-dependency for a full life.

1. **Make self-care a way of life:**

    The first thing a co-dependent loses sight of is themselves. A co-dependent is obsessed with pleasing the other person: catering to their whims, making their lives comfortable, providing for them. A co-dependent is a giver who has forgotten that giving should first be directed to oneself before others.

It is a common trait for co-dependents to expend energy, time, and resources 'fixing' the other person while they ignore their own needs. To break this cycle as a co-dependent, realize that you matter too.

a. **Take time to assess yourself and ask important questions.** What do you want from a relationship? What is your love language? How do you want your needs met? Sit down with a pen and a piece of paper and list your likes and dislikes. Explore the things you feel comfortable compromising on without sacrificing yourself in the process. It will help you to know when you start crossing that thin line between a loving, mutually-beneficial relationship and a co-dependency.

b. **Get to learn yourself.** Another common trait among co-dependents is that they hardly ever engage in recreational activities. To break away from co-dependency, you need to learn yourself. What activities make you happy? How would you love to spend your free time? What about the tennis you played in college? Would you love to take it up again?

Try out a lot of activities if you are not sure of what you like. Go for walks, go to the movies, take up gardening, register for an art/craft class, learn ice-skating, etc. By exploring many activities, you can decide on those you want to continue.

c. **Engage your senses.** Giving yourself sensual pleasure takes a back burner when you are focused on pleasing someone else. To be free from co-dependency, dedicate a block of time daily or weekly to pamper yourself. Put in your favorite album and just enjoy the melodies that make you happy, get a great book that everyone is raving about and sit down with a drink while traveling to another world/era through its pages. There are many ways to engage the senses so just pick the ones that call to you.

You may choose to luxuriate in a bubble bath with scented candles and light music, watch your favorite game on TV, or make time for meditation and yoga.

d. **Take care of your health.** As you determine to kiss co-dependency goodbye, start investing in your health and well-being.
- Commit to a physical fitness routine. This could take the form of taking up a gym membership, riding your bicycle daily, taking up yoga, going for runs, swimming, etc.
- Watch what you eat. The oft-used phrase 'you are what you eat', is very correct. Now is the time to ditch the junk foods for healthy, wholesome meals that nourish your body. Concentrate on whole grains, vegetables, legumes, nuts

and seeds, fruits, and some animal protein. Make sure each of the major food groups is represented each time you sit down to a meal.
- Sleep. The time spent sleeping is used by your body to carry out repairs in all the cells and tissues that need it. While the amount of sleep needed by each individual differs, you should have at least 6 hours of sound sleep every night. Poor sleep habit is linked to many diseases including depression, stroke, and heart disease.

    To fall asleep quicker and enjoy good quality sleep, don't consume caffeine or caffeinated products after 2 pm, reduce your exposure to blue light at night (stop using your phone/TV two hours before bed, use blackout curtains in the bedroom). Make your bedroom as relaxing as you can and avoid artificial lights or any form of distraction in the room.

2. **Learn independence:**

    Most co-dependents are scared of doing things by themselves or for themselves. Without the crutch of someone else to take care of, co-dependents are lost. You must learn to enjoy your own company. To learn independence, here are some things you can do.

    - Get to know yourself. Learning to know yourself is the first thing to do. To do this, start with journaling. You may choose to journal in the morning and set your intentions for the day. Then at the end of the day, write down the things that happened throughout the day, reflect on the things that happened, note areas where you need to make a change. Examine the areas where you compromised on your stand or said yes to things that you didn't want to do.

- Question your beliefs. We live in a conformist society such that we hardly question beliefs or take on issues. Questioning the things you believe in and why you believe in them is a valid way of knowing the things that truly serve you and discarding the things that do not. Do not be afraid to be the lone voice in a crowd for something that matters to you.

  When you question your beliefs and can stand by your convictions, you will not be afraid to hold an original thought.

- Be assertive. By becoming assertive, you get to improve not only the way you see yourself but the way that other people see you. Your self-esteem will, in turn, improve and you will gain a degree of autonomy. You can become more assertive through practice. Start by setting healthy boundaries and sticking to them, be willing to say no to the things that do not serve you, communicate your feelings and needs to family and friends. This will make your feelings validated.
- Make decisions for yourself. Realize that you are your own CEO; you determine the course of your own life. Living in a co-dependent relationship may have robbed you of being able to make decisions for yourself as the

things you do have always been for others. Something as little as deciding how you want to spend your day is a way of building your 'decision muscle.' Consider your wants and needs in every decision you make.

- Your needs matter. Your needs have been ignored for too long, now is the time to focus on them. Identify the things that satisfy you emotionally, spiritually, physically, and mentally. Do not be ashamed of needing a break or vacation, recognize that feeling lonely is a human emotion and do something about it (you can call up a friend for a dinner date if you need someone to talk to).

- Soothe yourself. Own your feelings, they are nothing to be ashamed of. Do not ignore them or counter them. Rather, do something that will make you feel better whenever you are down. Be in tune with yourself and take steps to rejuvenate yourself whenever you feel out of sorts.

3. **Be realistic with your expectations:**

   A co-dependent sees others as the source/reason for their happiness. This is a mindset you have to do away with in breaking the cycle of co-dependency. Let there be a mind shift as you accept that you are responsible for your happiness; your joy is not tied to what others do or choose to do. Do not expect to find fulfillment in other people. Be kind to yourself. Do not strive for perfection because that is a sure recipe for disillusionment. Forgive yourself daily—of your co-dependency, chances you never took, and ways you have derailed from your goals. Then realize that you will not become that assured and independent person you wish for in a single day but would get there with little changes here and there.

> To be happier, revitalize all the support network you have abandoned while in a co-dependent relationship. Family and friends are important to the overall sum of our happiness and spending quality time with them will surely make you happier. Be creative with activities instead of going to the same boring coffee shop week after week: join a book club, visit museums around you, tour your city like a tourist, become an informal food critic and sample the foods from different restaurants. There are so many things you can do either with

family and friends or by yourself if you only think about it.

4. **Start setting boundaries:**

    Co-dependency may as well be synonymous with a lack of boundaries. After allowing so many influences into your life for so long, it is important to regain your ability to say 'no' to the things that do not bring you joy.

    Realize that it is your and a way of watching out for your mental health by having set boundaries in every relationship. It does not matter whether these relationships involve your parents, friends, family, co-workers, or boss- certain boundaries must be in place. It means that you must be vocal about them: let the people around you know the things that you are comfortable with and those that you are not. Guide your personal space, body, emotions, possessions, time, beliefs, and values from influences that do not serve you. With appropriate boundaries in place, your self-esteem will improve. It also allows you to see yourself as a priority (as it should be). You realize that all of your needs are valid, be it to pursue a career, have your emotional needs met, or practice self-care. But you also want to make sure that you are not too rigid when it comes to boundaries. You don't want to isolate yourself from others by being uncompromising, but protect your interests and mental health.

5. **Make an assessment of your past:**

    A lot of co-dependents became that way as a result of past trauma, usually from familial dysfunction while growing up. But to heal and move on, you need to face this past and deal with it. Blocking it out or avoiding it will not make the pains go away. Whether you have been a victim of abuse, neglect, or abandonment, it is time to move. Here are steps to take to help heal from childhood trauma:

    a. **Get grounded.** To be grounded is to be fully present and aware of everything around you. Look for a quiet place that is free of distractions and disturbances. Sit down and close your eyes. Then take deep breaths, visualizing the pure air moving from your nostrils through your lungs to your stomach. Repeatedly contract and relax your muscles. Feel the connection to the earth beneath your feet as energy moves from your body to the earth. Move on to the next step.

b. **Bring back the event(s).** Look for a situation that made you upset some time back. Review it in details, feeling all the feelings associated with the event, even those you might have blocked out when it occurred. This is not the time to channel your anger or sadness or shame or pain but to allow yourself to feel them in the raw.

c. **Sense it.** While breathing deeply, allow your body and muscles that have tightened up to relax. Scan your body for the way you feel and take note of the attached physical responses—tightness, burning in your throat, etc. Say it to yourself, e.g. "My throat feels so tight I think I'm going to choke." Do not suppress the way you feel but describe each of them and accept them.

d. **Give it a name.** Name the emotion that caused each sensation. If the constriction in your throat is due to anger, name it. If your tight chest is caused by anxiety, do not be afraid to call it what it is.

e. **Love your emotions.** We have been brought up to believe that emotions are signs of weakness and should be done away with as soon as we feel them so this may be a little difficult to do but you have to love your emotions. Realize that they are a part of you, a part of your history and who you are today. It may sound ridiculous to say "I love myself for feeling sad about this even," but say it anyway. Do this irrespective of how low or difficult your emotions may be.

f. **Feel your feelings.** Do not rush through this process. Stay with the emotions and the way they make you feel. Do not shrink or hide from them. Rather, assess them. Acknowledge any attendant discomfort, they will pass but your healing lies in allowing yourself to feel them. Cry if you want to, scream and rage if that is the way to find release. If you need to use some expletives to express the way you feel, do it with the door shut and find relief.

g. **Learn from it.** What do your feelings tell you about what you have been through? Get a journal and write about what it all means to you. Take the lessons from them all.

h. **Share it.** If you are seeing a therapist or have someone you trust, you can share your observations with them. Explain what happened when the incident occurred and how you reacted. Let them know the shift in perspective you have now from the advantage of distance and age. For example, if your mother had always called you ugly while growing up which made you have poor body image issues, you may say: "I realize now that my mother calling me ugly while young was her way of reacting to my father's repeated infidelities. She was in so much pain that she needed to hurt someone else and she turned to me. I no longer see myself as ugly and especially appreciate my deep blue eyes and my smile,"

i. **Let go of it.** Use any means you desire to let go of the emotion. It may be a symbolic act like burning a letter you wrote to the one that hurt you or you may take a shower to denote the feeling and all its pain leaving your body with the water moving down the drain.

> Now you are free. Live in that freedom and enjoy your life.

6. **Get therapy or counseling:**

    The truth is that if you have been in a co-dependent relationship, your emotions have been affected and your views about relationships skewed. This is why you need therapy even when you might feel that you can do without it. As you aim to move forward with your life, therapy will help you develop ways of interaction with other people that are healthy for you.

    Here are ways therapy/counseling can help you break free from a co-dependent relationship:

a. As an objective party, a therapist will help you identify any co-dependent tendencies you may possess. You will begin to see all your actions in a new light and be able to avoid the things that may make you go into an unhealthy relationship again. And if your co-dependency is tied to past trauma, they can help you understand how co-dependent patterns develop.

b. A co-dependent person usually gives kindness to others but themselves. Therapy will help you learn how to be compassionate to yourself, how to forgive yourself of past mistakes, and how to work around your inadequacies. As you learn kindness to self, you will feel less need to overcompensate through co-dependency.

c. A therapist will also help you develop healthy relationships moving forward. You will learn how to be supportive to people without neglecting yourself or enabling unsavory behavior. You will learn the power in assertiveness and how to claim agency over your own life even while in relationships.

d. A therapist will help you realize the [power of 'no.' no is one of the most difficult words for a co-dependent to say yet one of the most freeing. Your inability to say no may have led to mental, physical, and emotional burnout becoming a part of your life. Seeing a therapist will help you get your power back—you do not have to be a 'yes' person to be loved, your own needs should be met too, you get to spend your time on the things that serve you and make you happy.

7. **Choose new relationships with care:** The first thing you need to realize is that you do not have to go into another (romantic) relationship after leaving a co-dependency. Do not be afraid to stay alone and take time to build other non-romantic relationships that are essential to your well-being. But if you choose to start another relationship, pick someone that has high self-esteem. Do not be with someone needy, jealous, or controlling. Be sure that your new partner supports you having a full life that may involve friends or recreational activities they are not interested in.

Here are important points to keep in mind before going into a new relationship.

a. You are your number one love. Do not go into a relationship to find love. Love yourself and accept that it is enough even if you never find someone else to love you the way you deserve to be loved. Love your body; all its flaws and beauty. Listen to it and respect its needs. Love yourself mentally (silence every negative thought that makes you feel inadequate), emotionally, and spiritually.

b. Go into a relationship for the right reasons. Ask yourself the hard questions about why you are going into a relationship with a particular person. Be sure your prospective partner is committed to having an equal relationship free of drama and filled with kindness and care.

c. Go for someone that makes you laugh. No, you don't have to date Trevor Noah. But go for someone you can have fun with. If the person makes you feel like a goofy kid again, they are likely to be good for you.

You can live a full, happy life after co-dependency. All you have to do is be ready to put in the work to move on from your past. Be ready to invest in the things that serve you and increase your happiness and set boundaries that allow you to maintain your peace of mind. One day at a time, you can conscientiously break free from co-dependency and enjoy healthy relationships.

Other Books by The Same Author

Change Your Life: How to Overcome Anxiety, Depression and Negative Thinking

How to Deal with Difficult People: Control the Situation! Overcome Your Annoying and Frustrating Coworkers, Friends, Parents, or Classmates

How to Overcome Shyness and Social Anxiety: Deal with Stage Fright, Fear of Public Speaking, Social Phobia, And Ultimately Gain New Confidence

How to Deal with Rejection: Powerful Ways to Restore Social Confidence, Attract Better Opportunities, And Take Charge of Your Environment

How to Deal with A Narcissist: Best Ways to Respond to A Narcissist, Confront Self-Important People, And Thrive Efficiently

Printed in Great Britain
by Amazon